# WHEELS AND AXLES
## IN MY
## MAKERSPACE

by Tim Miller and
Rebecca Sjonger

CRABTREE
Publishing Company
www.crabtreebooks.com

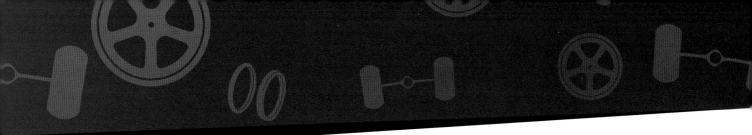

*For Caleb, Micah, and Nathaniel*

**Authors:** Tim Miller, Rebecca Sjonger

**Series research and development:**
Reagan Miller

**Editorial director:** Kathy Middleton

**Editor:** Janine Deschenes

**Design:** Margaret Amy Salter

**Proofreader:** Petrice Custance

**Photo research:** Margaret Amy Salter

**Production coordinator and prepress technician:**
Margaret Amy Salter

**Print coordinator:** Margaret Amy Salter

**Photographs:**

Shutterstock: © Art Konovalov p13 (bottom)

Wikimedia: Welcome Images p24 (inset)

Craig Culliford: pp8-9

All other images by Shutterstock

**Library and Archives Canada Cataloguing in Publication**

Miller, Tim, 1973-, author
      Wheels and axles in my makerspace / Tim Miller, Rebecca Sjonger.

(Simple machines in my makerspace)
Includes index.
Issued in print and electronic formats.
ISBN 978-0-7787-3375-1 (hardcover).--
ISBN 978-0-7787-3383-6 (softcover).--
ISBN 978-1-4271-1905-6 (HTML)

    1. Wheels--Juvenile literature. 2. Axles--Juvenile literature.
3. Makerspaces--Juvenile literature. I. Sjonger, Rebecca, author II. Title.

TJ181.5.M56 2017        j621.8        C2016-907452-8
                                  C2016-907453-6

**Library of Congress Cataloging-in-Publication Data**

Names: Miller, Tim, 1973- author. | Sjonger, Rebecca, author.
Title: Wheels and axles in my makerspace / Tim Miller and Rebecca Sjonger.
Description: New York, New York : Crabtree Publishing Company, [2017] |
   Series: Simple machines in my makerspace | Audience: Ages 8-11. |
   Audience: Grades 4 to 6. | Includes index.
Identifiers: LCCN 2016054111 (print) | LCCN 2016056161 (ebook) |
   ISBN 9780778733751 (reinforced library binding : alk. paper) |
   ISBN 9780778733836 (pbk. : alk. paper) |
   ISBN 9781427119056 (Electronic HTML)
Subjects: LCSH: Wheels--Juvenile literature. | Simple machines--Juvenile
   literature. | Makerspaces--Juvenile literature.
Classification: LCC TJ181.5 .M56 2017 (print) | LCC TJ181.5 (ebook) |
   DDC 621.8/11--dc23
LC record available at https://lccn.loc.gov/2016054111

## Crabtree Publishing Company

www.crabtreebooks.com     1-800-387-7650

Printed in Canada/032017/BF20170111

**Published in Canada**
**Crabtree Publishing**
616 Welland Ave.
St. Catharines, Ontario
L2M 5V6

**Published in the United States**
**Crabtree Publishing**
PMB 59051
350 Fifth Avenue, 59th Floor
New York, New York 10118

**Published in the United Kingdom**
**Crabtree Publishing**
Maritime House
Basin Road North, Hove
BN41 1WR

**Published in Australia**
**Crabtree Publishing**
3 Charles Street
Coburg North
VIC 3058

# CONTENTS

# YOU CAN BE A MAKER!

A maker is a person who dreams up new ways to solve problems and create things. They learn by experimenting and following their interests. Makers see how to use everyday items in creative ways. Do you think you can think like a maker? Keep reading and get ready to create fun ways to lift, roll, and move things.

## TEAMWORK

Makers know that working together helps them create amazing things. Teaming up with other makers means that you can share creative ideas, skills, and supplies. Working in a group also helps you to be open to other points of view and new directions. **Makerspaces** are places where makers work together. Makerspaces can be everywhere—from your school, to your local library, to your home! You can set up your own makerspace and invite your friends to join you.

# A new way of learning

There is no right or wrong way to make something.
Makers know that:

✓ The only limit is your imagination.

✓ Every idea or question—even ones that seem silly—
could lead to something amazing.

✓ Each team member adds value to a project.

✓ Things do not always go as planned. This is part of being a maker!
Challenges help us think creatively.

# WHAT ARE WHEELS AND AXLES?

What do cars, Ferris wheels, and fishing rod reels have in common? They all use wheels and axles! A wheel and an axle work together. The wheel can be a solid disk or a circle-shaped frame with spokes. Spokes are small bars that fit between the center of a wheel and its outside rim. The axle is a straight, solid rod. It goes through the center of the wheel.

## SIMPLE MACHINES

A wheel and axle is a **simple machine**. Simple machines are tools with few or no moving parts. We use them to change the amount or direction of a **force**. Force is the **effort** needed to push or pull on an object.

## HELP WITH WORK

Simple machines make **work** easier, faster, or safer. Work is the use of force to move an object from one place to another. A wheel and axle can help move a load, change the direction a load is moving, or change its speed. A wheel and axle can also roll over a surface with less effort.

## WHEELS AND AXLES IN ACTION

Where have you seen wheels and axles in action? They have many different uses! For example, a pottery wheel spins a piece of clay in circles. The same simple machine helps a skateboarder flip some tricks at a skate park.

*Two wheels and one axle make up one wheel and axle set. A skateboard has two sets of wheels and axles.*

# MAKE A WHEEL AND AXLE

Building a small car will help you understand how sets of wheels and axles work together to move loads along a straight path, with little effort. You will learn how the total weight of the load is spread over each wheel. This will help you with the maker missions in this book.

## Materials

- **Four spools of the same size, or other round objects of the same size such as bottle caps, to use as wheels**
- **Two straws**
- **Two wooden skewers to use as axles**
- **Clay or sticky tack**
- **One styrofoam block, small cardboard box, or other object to use as the body of the car (this is the load)**
- **Tape**

## SET IT UP!

1. Push one wooden skewer through a straw so that the skewer sticks out at least 2 inches (5 cm) on both ends of the straw. If your wheels are large you may need to leave more space. If needed, cut the straw so that the skewer sticks out far enough.
2. Repeat step one using the second wooden skewer and straw.

3. Push the end of a skewer through the center of a spool.
4. Cover the ends of the skewer with clay or sticky tack to keep the spool on the skewer.

rim

5. Repeat steps three and four with the remaining spools and ends of skewers.

6. Use tape to attach the body of the car to your two sets of wheels and axles. Tape the center of each straw to the bottom of the block or box.

7. Give the car a push and watch how it moves.

> Axles connect wheels and keep them stable, or steady, as they roll.

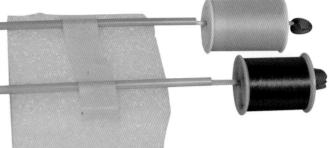

# Think About It

Does your car move in a smooth, straight path? If not, how can you improve it?

The weight of the load should be spread equally over the four wheels. Why do you think this is important?

Try repeating this experiment with other wheels of different shapes and sizes. How did this change how your car moved?

Once you understand how a simple machine works, you will be able to modify, or change it, to solve different problems. How you build each wheel and axle will change based on the criteria of each maker mission. For example, the materials, size, or type of load may change from challenge to challenge. Check out the "Modify Your Machine" boxes throughout the book.

# MAKER TIPS

Are you ready to get moving with wheels and axles? Each of the maker projects in this book helps you get creative and use your simple machine in new ways. It's helpful to start each project by brainstorming. Take five minutes and, by yourself or with other makers, come up with as many ideas as you can. Always respect the ideas of others.

When you have a list of ideas, pick the one you think might work best and make a plan to carry it out. Sketch out how each part of your project should look and measure everything carefully. Remember that although you may make a good plan, things can change as you go. Be open-minded to change and see where your project ends up!

# Helpful hints

Running into problems is part of the maker process. If you are stuck, try some of the following tips:

- Think about solutions to problems or challenges you have solved in the past. There may be some parts you could add to or change to help you solve this problem or challenge.

- Look at your list of ideas. **Ask:** Can we combine two or more ideas into one?

- Think about each part of your problem or challenge. **Ask:** Is there a certain part or area that is not working?

- State how you will know if you have solved the problem or challenge. Fill in the blank: I will know I have solved the problem when _____.

- Delete or Double Up! **Ask:** What would happen if we removed this part? What would happen if we added another of the same part?

# MOVE A LOAD

Can you name three things that have wheels and axles? Think about how each of them is used. Likely, they move objects or people. People mainly use wheels and axles to make moving loads faster, easier, and safer.

## LIGHTEN THE LOAD

Look around your neighborhood and you will see many kinds of transportation that use wheels and axles. For example, you might see someone pulling a child in a wagon. The wheels and axles roll the load of the child easily. This saves the person who is pulling from having to lift and carry the child down the street!

## HOW DOES IT WORK?

Multiple wheels help carry heavy loads. The total weight spreads over each wheel. A wagon has two sets of wheels and axles—one at the front, and one at the back. Each set is made up of a pair of wheels that connect to one axle that spreads across the width of the wagon. The wheels and axles attach to the bottom of the wagon. They must be able to spin freely for the wagon to move. Adding a handle makes the work of moving a load even easier and faster.

## TRY IT!

Flip to the next page to get started on making your own wheeled load mover. Begin by making plans for each part of your project. Consider brainstorming ideas with some friends!

handle

axle

wheel

Some tractor-trailers have 18 or more wheels. These trucks can move loads weighing up to 80,000 pounds (36,287 kg)!

# MAKE IT MOVE

Are you ready to roll? Use at least two wheels and one axle to move a load. Your creation must carry your load at least 5 feet (152 cm) in distance. The load must include at least one heavy book and one toy.

## Materials

- Paper
- Pencil
- Measuring tape or ruler
- 2 or more wheels
- 1 or more axles
- Glue, tape, etc.
- A box for the body, such as a cereal box
- Something to use as a handle, such as a skipping rope
- Book and toy

## MODIFY YOUR MACHINE

The load you must move is much bigger than the one on pages 8-9. You may need to find or build bigger wheels.

# THINK ABOUT IT

**Design**

How will you attach the axle to the cart body so that it is able to turn?

Is it possible to attach a tube in which you insert the axle?

Would it help to add holes in the sides?

Draw as many ideas as possible to show what your wheeled mover might look like.

What difference will adding a handle make?

How could you attach a handle?

**Size**

How long will your axle need to be?

## MISSION ACCOMPLISHED

Test your creation and note the results. Did you carry at least one book and one toy a distance of 5 feet (152 cm)? If not, what could you try next?

When you are happy with your project, flip to page 30 for more maker ideas.

# SMOOTH ROLLERS

Rollers make the work of creating a smooth surface faster and easier. A roller, such as the type used for baking or flattening roads, is actually a wheel and axle! The wheel moves a heavy force across a bumpy surface. This leaves the rolled surface flat and smooth.

## ON A ROLL

Some rollers are huge! A roller attached to a tractor can be used on roads. It rolls over many uneven road surfaces and uses a lot of force to make them smooth. Other rollers work in smaller spaces. Have you ever used a rolling pin on a lumpy mound of dough? It is much faster and easier to roll out the dough than it is to flatten it with your hands.

> Large wheels travel more easily over bumpy surfaces than smaller wheels do.

## HOW DOES IT WORK?

A roller has one very wide wheel. It attaches to a long axle. Some rollers have handles—usually the two ends of the axle sticking out of the wheel. This is the case with most rolling pins. The handles (axle) make it easier to roll the wheel. The person using the rolling pin holds onto the handles and presses down to roll forward or backward.

handle

handle

## TRY IT!

Make your own roller to try this out for yourself. Get started with the Make It Roll challenge on the next page. Use your imagination and see what you can create!

# MAKE IT ROLL

Get ready for some flattening fun! Make a rolling pin using one wheel and one axle. Your creation must smooth one container of play dough into a flattened disk.

## Materials

- Paper
- Pencil
- Wide wheel, such as a pool noodle
- Long axle, such as a wooden dowel
- Play dough

## MODIFY YOUR MACHINE

Your wheel needs to be very wide—and the axle even wider. Look back at the description of rolling pins on pages 16 and 17 for help.

# THINK ABOUT IT

**Materials**

What can you find around your home that you could use as materials? Get creative!

**Design**

How will you make sure the wheel does not stick to the play dough?

Should the axle rotate along with the wheel?

## MISSION ACCOMPLISHED

It is time to see if your roller can smooth out a lump of play dough. If it did not work as planned, what could you try next? Once your roller is a smoothing simple machine, try something new with it.

**Check out Endless Ideas on page 30.**

# POWER LIFTING

Most wheels and axles move loads. Many of these wheels and axles are on transportation such as trucks or wagons. But one kind of wheel and axle moves a load without ever touching the ground! They move loads by lifting them.

## WHEELS, AXLES, AND WELLS

Have you ever seen a bucket of water lifted out of a well? Someone may have hauled on a long rope to pull up the full bucket. Or that person may have turned an axle to wind the rope up onto a wheel. This simple machine makes raising and lowering objects faster and easier.

## HOW DOES IT WORK?

The bucket attaches to one end of the rope. The other end attaches to a wheel with a wide rim. The axle inside the wheel sticks out to create a turning handle. Turning the axle in one direction winds the rope around the axle and raises the bucket. Turning it in the opposite direction unwinds the rope and lowers the bucket.

## TRY IT!

Make your own lifter using a wheel and axle to see how this simple machine works. Gather some friends to work together and share your ideas! Get started with the challenge on the next page.

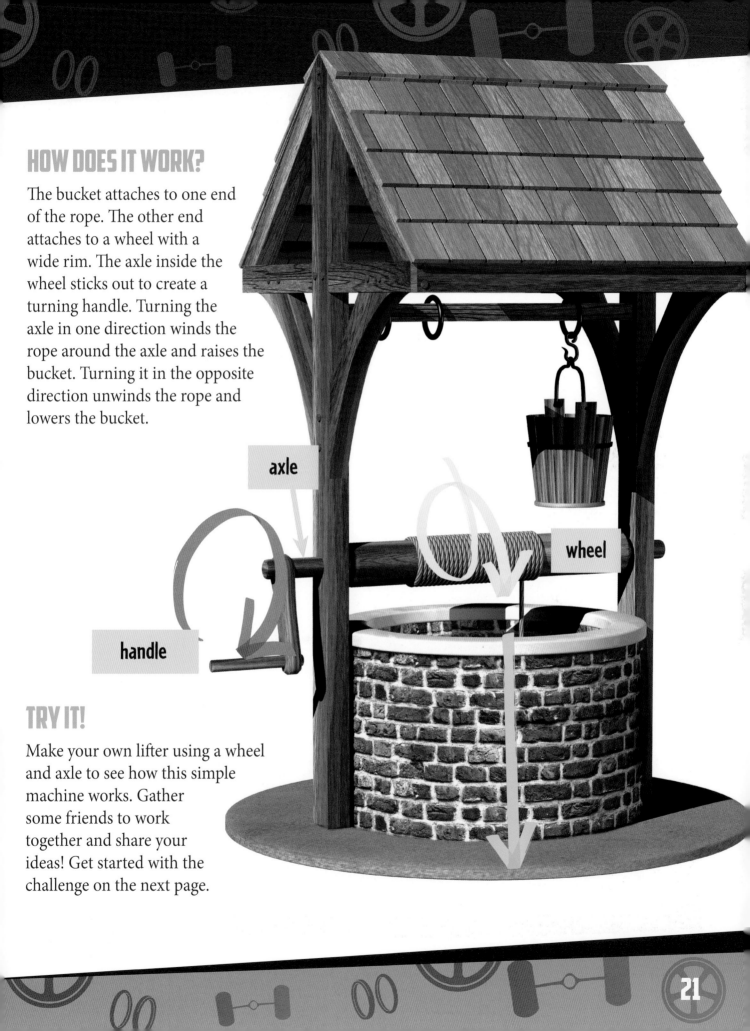

axle

wheel

handle

## MAKER MISSION

See for yourself how lifting a bucket from a well works—without getting wet! Use a wheel and axle to make a machine that can lift a load. Look back to the example of the well to figure out how your wheel and axle will be positioned. It must raise your school bag at least 1 foot (30.5 cm) off the ground.

## Materials

- Paper
- Pencil
- Measuring tape or ruler
- Wheel
- Axle
- Rope
- (Optional) Hook
- School bag

## MODIFY YOUR MACHINE

Did you do the Make It Roll challenge on pages 18-19? Think about how you could repurpose the wheel and axle for this project

# THINK ABOUT IT

**Design**

How will you attach your rope to the wheel and to the load?

How can you keep the rope from slipping on the wheel?

**?**

**?**

Will you use other materials, such as hooks?

**?**

Will wrapping the rope over top of itself help?

How much axle do you need to leave out on one end to make a handle for turning?

**Materials**

What could you add to the axle to make it easier to turn?

Is there something in your home or yard that might work to hold up the ends of the axle?

**?**

## MISSION ACCOMPLISHED

Test your lifter and see if it can raise your school bag at least 1 foot (30.5 cm) off the ground. If it does not, what could you try next?

Once you succeed at this challenge, go to page 30 for more maker ideas.

# USE THE WIND

Some wheels and axles are very clear to see—such as those on a motorcycle—and others aren't so obvious. For example, a windmill is actually a wheel and an axle! Unlike most other wheels and axles, windmills attach to a tall base that holds them high in the air.

## HOW DOES IT WORK?

As you can probably guess based on the name, windmills use wind as a source of power. A large wheel is shaped so that air blowing on it makes it move. The wheel attaches to an axle. The axle usually connects to a long pole, which acts as the base and raises it in the air to catch wind.

axle

## CONNECTED WHEELS AND AXLES

Wind turns the wheel, which then turns the axle. The axle attaches to parts inside of the base of the mill, including more wheels and axles. The force from the wind makes each part move. The earliest windmills made the work of grinding grain easier and faster. Today, these simple machines can help produce power for homes and businesses.

### TRY IT!

Are you ready to experiment with making your own wheel and axle that will move in the wind? Remember, makers are always up for a good challenge! Flip the page to get started.

**MAKER MISSION**

Get ready to start spinning! Make a wheel and axle that will turn in the wind. The wheel must make at least one full rotation.

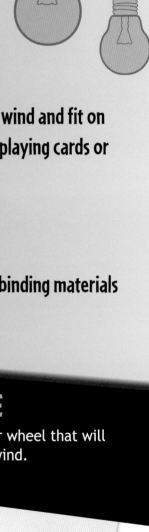

## Materials

- Paper
- Pencil
- Wheel
- Axle
- Objects that will move in the wind and fit on the rim of the wheel, such as playing cards or plastic spoons
- Pole
- Base for pole
- Glue, tape, elastics, or other binding materials
- Scissors

### MODIFY YOUR MACHINE

Add objects to the rim of your wheel that will help catch the power of the wind.

# THINK ABOUT IT

## Materials

Look around outdoors for possible poles that already have strong bases.

If you are working with a group, try to come up with as many ideas as possible and test them to see what works best.

## Design

How will you make sure that the axle can turn when it attaches to the pole?

How will you catch the air with the wheel, making it rotate? Draw some ideas.

### MISSION ACCOMPLISHED

Test your wind-powered creation. Is the wheel able to rotate in at least one full circle? Make notes about anything that you need to change.

Go to page 30 to find ways to make it even better.

# MORE MACHINES

There are five other kinds of simple machines. Have you ever seen the examples below making work easier, safer, or faster?

| NAME | PURPOSE | PICTURE | EXAMPLES |
|---|---|---|---|
| inclined planes | move objects between two heights | | water slide funnel wheelchair ramp |
| levers | move, lift, or lower objects | | seesaw scissors catapult |
| pulleys | lift, lower, or move objects; transfer force from one object to another | | flagpole zip line bicycle chain |
| screws | join, cut into, lift, or lower objects | | jar and lid drill light bulb |
| wedges | split apart or lift objects; stop objects from moving | | ax door stop shovel |

# COMPLEX MACHINES

Joining two or more simple machines creates a **complex machine**. A bicycle is a complex machine that combines wheels, axles, levers, pulleys, and screws to make the work of traveling easier. It also makes the work more fun!

## CHANGE IT UP!

How could you connect a wheel and axle with another simple machine to make a complex machine? Start by experimenting with one of the projects from this book. Flip to page 30 to get other ideas for your projects.

# ENDLESS IDEAS

Makers are always learning and coming up with new ideas! You could make each of the projects in this book in many different ways. For example:

## Make It Move (pages 14-15):

- How could your cart carry a bigger load?
- What other materials could you use for the body of the cart?

## Make It Roll (pages 18-19):

- Change it up! Try different wheel widths and weights to see how they affect the way your roller works.
- Could you roll out other soft materials?

## Make It Lift (pages 22-23):

- How could you modify your project to double the height of the first load you lifted?
- How could your project lift a heavier load?

## Make It Turn (pages 26-27):

- Move your project to the next level and put it to work! If your axle was longer, how could you use the spinning force to do a simple task? Hint: Think about connecting your axle to something else that moves or turns.

# LEARNING MORE

## BOOKS

Allyn, Daisy. *Wheels and Axles.* Gareth Stevens, 2013.

Bailey, Gerry. *Rolling Along: The Wheel and Axle.* Crabtree, 2014.

Challen, Paul. *Get to Know Wheels and Axles.* Crabtree, 2009.

Lamachia, Dawn. *Wheels and Axles at Work.* Enslow, 2015.

• • • • • • • • • • • • • • • • • • • • • • • • • • • •

## WEBSITES

Visit this web page to watch a video about wheels and axles.

**http://mocomi.com/wheel-and-axle/**

Find step-by-step instructions for making your own rubber band car at the PBS Kids website.

**http://pbskids.org/designsquad/parentseducators/resources/rubber_band_car.html**

Learn more about wheels and axles and how they work on this website.

**www.explainthatstuff.com/howwheelswork.html**

• • • • • • • • • • • • • • • • • • • • • • • • • • • •

# GLOSSARY

**axle** A straight, solid rod that goes through the center of a wheel

**brainstorming** Coming up with as many ideas as possible to solve a problem or answer a question

**complex machine** A machine that combines at least two simple machines

**effort** The amount of energy, or power, used to do something

**force** The effort needed to push or pull on an object

**makerspace** A place where makers work together and share their ideas and resources

**rim** The outer edge of a wheel

**simple machine** A tool with few or no moving parts that people use to change the amount or direction of a force

**spoke** A small bar that fits between the center of a wheel and its outside rim

**wheel** A solid disk or a circle-shaped frame with spokes

**windmill** A complex machine that uses power from wind to make other machines work

**work** The use of force to move an object from one place to another

# INDEX

## ABOUT THE AUTHORS

Tim Miller is a mechanical engineer who loves to work with his hands. He is also a founding board member of Fusion Labworks, a maker community. Rebecca Sjonger is the author of over 40 children's books, including three titles in the *Be a Maker!* series.